Excellent Point!

Written by
Jackie Monsour
Smith

a JackieMo BOOK

Illustrated by
Marcy Petricig
Braasch

With a friend at hand, you will see the light.
— Elton John

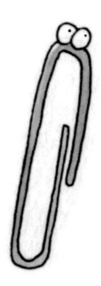

WGA registered 2112533 2021

All rights reserved. No part of this book may be used or reproduced in any manner whatsoever without written permission except in the case of brief quotations embodied in critical articles and reviews.
Printed in the United States of America

ISBN: 978-1-7351467-3-7

Published by JackieMo Books.

At least that's what she said, but deep down in her toes...

she knew the smile on her face
was really just for show.

Rock was her best friend,
so Scissors felt confused.
Was she angry? Was she jealous?
She didn't like to lose.

"I have an idea!" Scissors shouted to herself.

Now each and every time Scissors ever loses, she quickly tells the crowd all of her excuses.

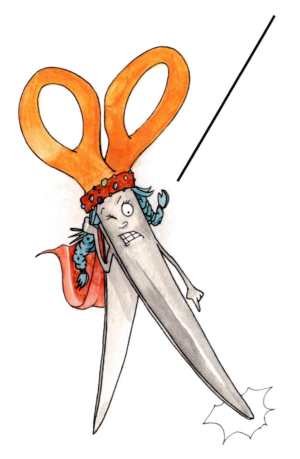

Scissors looked around
for pity from her friends,
but all she saw were rolling eyes,
so she thought and thought again.

"I have an idea!"
Scissors shouted to herself.

Scissors always knew that Rock had confidence. She thought putting Rock down slightly was of no consequence.

So, Scissors spread some rumors, choosing words that were unkind, whispering cruel things in every ear that she could find.

"Why does Rock always wear that headband? It doesn't even match her cape."

Scissors noticed quickly, and thought it rather weird, that neighbors ran the other way whenever she appeared.

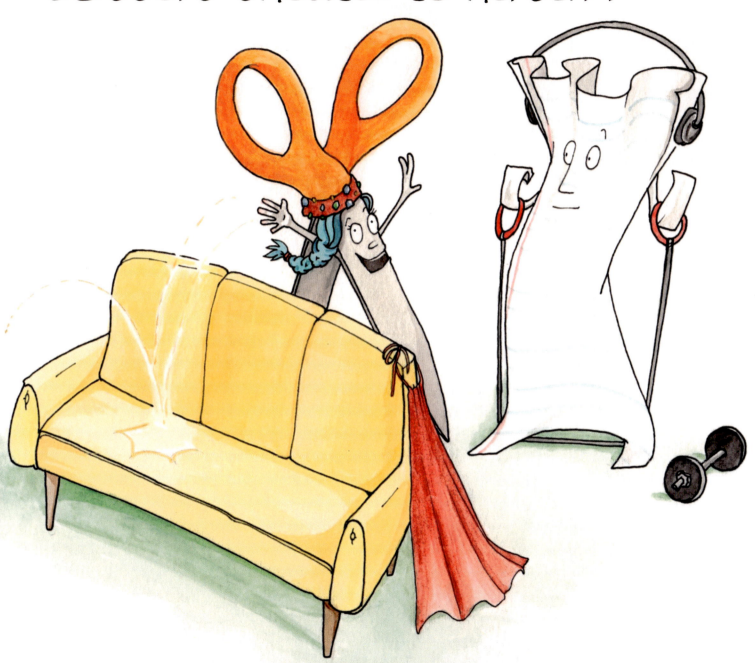

Scissors threw a party, with games and food and fun.

She made the greatest effort, asking everyone to come.

BUT, only if they promised to never choose the Rock. Scissors waited patiently, then really got a shock!

She finally kicked Rock out!
And it would be forever.

She smiled
kind of crooked,
feeling proud to be so clever.

Scissors took home trophies by oodles, piles, and stacks. The challenge was so easy, she could finally relax.

Scissors ran her finger across her skinny blade. Her sharp edge, used for cutting, had now begun to fade.

She tried to cut

but her medal-winning blades
sat there useless, dull, and drab.

and slice with a jab and then a stab,

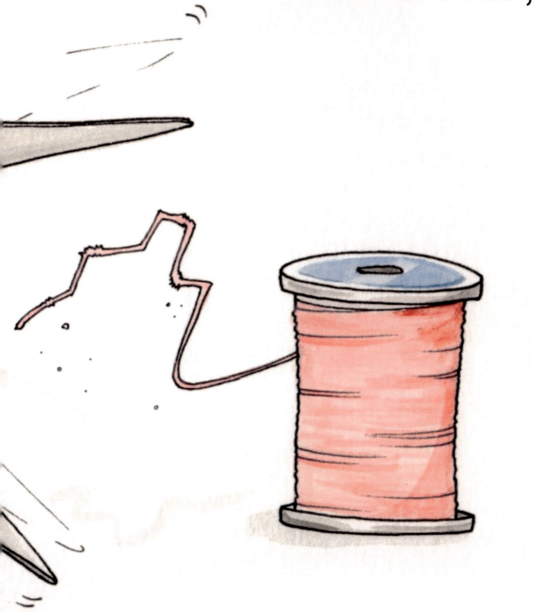

She cried, well, just a little. Ok, she cried a lot!
Wondering how she ended up
in such an awful spot.

Paper let her cry it out while folding all the socks, saying, "If you let me do it, I'm going to call Rock."

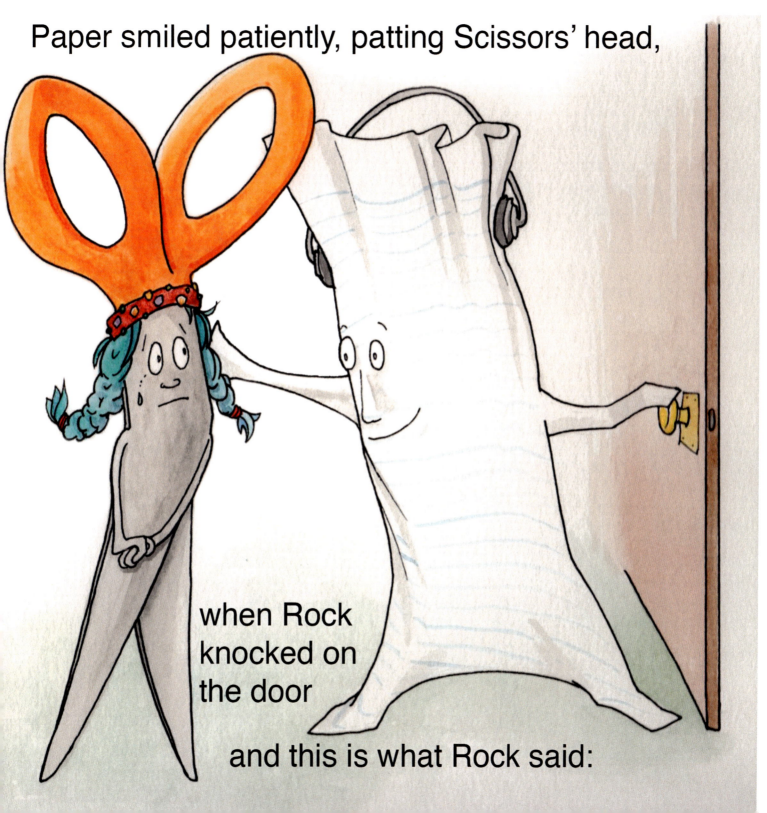

*Some rocks are used to sharpen blades by running the blade along the rock. Rocks near water make good sharpening stones because they are smooth.

Scissors grew a smile that she thought would burst her cheeks. Crazy as it sounds, it lasted weeks and weeks and weeks.

Rock, Paper, Scissors are back to being friends and friendship's so much better when your smile is genuine.

Made in the USA
Las Vegas, NV
27 April 2021